Seasons

D1712396

Contents

Picking Apples in Fall

Gil and his family
live in New York City.

It is fall.
Gil and his family
visit an apple farm
in the country.

5

Gil picks red, yellow, and green apples.

"Can I eat an apple?"
asked Gil.
"Yes, you can eat
an apple," said Mom.

Gil eats an apple.

The baby wants
an apple, too!

Gil and his family
drive home.

Gil makes applesauce.
"I'm making applesauce
for the baby!"
said Gil.

Growing Corn
Through the Seasons

In spring farmers prepare the soil. They plant corn seeds.

In summer and fall, farmers
gather the corn.
They sell it
at the market.

Four Seasons

It snows in winter.

It rains in spring.

It's sunny in summer.

It's windy in fall.

Fall Leaves

You can make fall leaves.
You need these things.

a leaf

scissors

a pencil

colored paper

Draw 3 leaves.

Cut out 3 leaves.

One leaf is orange.

That means $\frac{1}{3}$ of

the leaves are orange.

go
sledding

build
snowmen

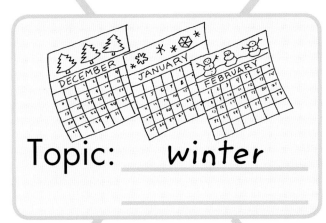

Topic: ___ winter ___

drink
hot chocolate

read
by fire

Winter

Winter is my favorite season. I go sledding. I build snowmen with my friends, too. Hot chocolate tastes good in winter. Papa and I like to read by the fire. Winter is fun!

Choose a topic to write about.
Write the topic
in the middle box
of your web.
Fill in your web and use
it to help you write.

Topic: *spring*

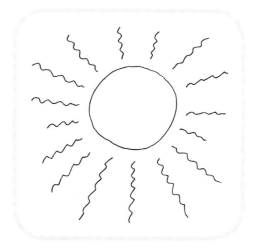

Topic: *summer*

Topic: *fall*

Topic: *winter*